·Cooking for Today·

MEXICAN COOKING

·Cooking for Today·

MEXICAN COOKING

ROSEMARY WADEY

SMITHMARK

This edition published in 1996 by SMITHMARK Publishers,
a division of U.S. Media Holdings Inc.
16 East 32nd Street, New York, NY 10016.

SMITHMARK books are available for bulk purchase for sales promotion and premium use.
For details write or call the manager of special sales, SMITHMARK Publishers,
16 East 32nd Street, New York, NY 10016; (212) 532-6600.

Produced by Haldane Mason, London
for
Parragon Book Service Ltd
Unit 13–17
Avonbridge Trading Estate
Atlantic Road
Avonmouth
Bristol BS11 9QD

ISBN 0-7651-9853-3

Printed in Italy

1 0 9 8 7 6 5 4 3 2 1

Acknowledgements
Art Direction: Ron Samuels
Editor: Joanna Swinnerton
Series Design: Pedro & Frances Prá-Lopez, Kingfisher Design, London
Page Design: F14 Creative Consultants
Photography and styling: Sue Atkinson
Home Economist: Rosemary Wadey

Photographs on pages 6, 20, 32, 44 & 62 reproduced by permission of ZEFA Picture Library (UK) Ltd.

Note:
Cup measurements in this book are for American cups. Tablespoons are assumed to be 15ml.
Unless otherwise stated, milk is assumed to be full-fat, eggs are AA extra large and pepper is freshly ground black pepper.

Contents

CHAPTER ONE

Soups & Appetizers

Most Mexican food has a "bite" to it because of the liberal use of chilis in one form or another, and soups and appetizers are no exception. Soups are generally served at all main meals, and they are usually fairly substantial, being full of beans and vegetables and having a certain zip from the addition of chilis, some variety of chili sauce, or Tabasco. They also make excellent snacks and light meals when served with rustic bread or rolls or, of course, tortillas – the Mexican form of bread that is served with almost everything.

Tortillas are made from either masa harina (a maize meal) or wheat flour, which are similar but offer slight differences in color, texture, and flavor. The wheat tortillas have the advantage of being a little easier to handle.

Typical Mexican appetizers include dips made with such ingredients as avocados and roasted pumpkin seeds. Small pieces of tortilla or shaped tortillas are fried or baked and topped with a variety of ingredients including shellfish, cheese, meat, and poultry. Eggs, seafood, vegetables, and fruit also feature widely. Guacamole makes a splendid appetizer served as a dip, though it also features in many of the other recipes as an accompaniment.

Opposite: *A street stall in Oaxaca, in the south of Mexico.*

STEP 1

STEP 2

STEP 3

STEP 4

VEGETABLE & GARBANZO BEAN SOUP

A good tasty soup full of vegetables, chicken, and garbanzo beans with just a hint of spiciness to serve on any occasion.

SERVES 4–6

3 tbsp olive oil
1 large onion, finely chopped
2–3 crushed garlic cloves
$\frac{1}{2}$–1 red chili, deseeded and very finely chopped (see page 24)
1 chicken breast (about 5 ounces)
2 celery stalks, finely chopped
1$\frac{1}{4}$ cups coarsely grated carrots
5 cups chicken stock
2 bay leaves
$\frac{1}{2}$ tsp dried oregano
$\frac{1}{4}$ tsp ground cinnamon
salt and pepper
14 ounce can garbanzo beans, drained
8 ounces tomatoes, peeled, deseeded, and chopped
1 tbsp tomato paste
chopped fresh cilantro or parsley, to garnish

1 Heat the oil in a large saucepan, and fry the onion, garlic, and chili over a low heat until softened but not colored.

2 Slice the chicken breast thickly, and add to the saucepan. Continue to cook the chicken until it is well sealed all over.

3 Add the celery, carrots, stock, bay leaves, oregano, cinnamon, and seasoning to the saucepan. Bring to a boil, and then cover the pan. Simmer gently for about 20 minutes, or until the chicken is tender.

4 Remove the chicken from the soup, and chop it finely, or cut it into narrow strips.

5 Return the chicken to the pan with the garbanzo beans, tomatoes, and tomato paste and cover the pan.

6 Simmer for an additional 15–20 minutes. Discard the bay leaves, and adjust the seasoning. Serve very hot, sprinkled with cilantro or parsley and with warmed tortillas to accompany it.

DRIED GARBANZO BEANS

Dried garbanzo beans may be used instead of canned. Soak overnight in cold water, then drain and cook in fresh water for about 1 hour until tender.

STEP 2

STEP 4

STEP 6

STEP 6

BEAN SOUP

Beans feature widely in Mexican cooking, and here pinto beans are cooked with a mixture of vegetables to give a spicy soup with an interesting texture. Serve with tortillas or crusty bread.

SERVES 4

$^3/_4$ *cup pinto beans*
5 cups water
1$^1/_4$–1$^1/_2$ cups carrots, finely chopped
1 large onion, finely chopped
2–3 garlic cloves, crushed
$^1/_2$–1 chili, deseeded and finely chopped (see page 24)
4 cups chicken or vegetable stock
2 tomatoes, peeled and finely chopped
2 celery stalks, very thinly sliced
salt and pepper
1 tbsp chopped fresh cilantro (optional)

CROUTONS:
3 slices white bread
fat or oil for deep-frying
1–2 garlic cloves, crushed

1 Soak the beans overnight in cold water; drain and put in a pan with the water. Bring to a boil and boil fast for 10 minutes. Cover and simmer for 2 hours, or until the beans are tender, and most of the liquid has evaporated.

2 Add the carrots, onion, garlic, chili, and stock, and bring back to a boil. Cover and simmer for an additional 30 minutes until very tender.

3 Remove half the beans and vegetables with the cooking juices, and press through a strainer, or purée in a food processor or blender until smooth.

4 Return the bean purée to the saucepan, and add the tomatoes and celery to the soup. Simmer for an additional 10–15 minutes, or until the celery is just tender, adding a little more stock or water if the soup is too thick.

5 Add seasoning to taste, and stir in the chopped cilantro, if using. Serve with the croûtons.

6 To make the croûtons, remove the crusts from the bread and cut into small cubes. Heat the oil with the garlic in a small skillet, and fry the cubes until golden-brown. Drain on paper towels. The croûtons may be made up to 48 hours in advance, and stored in an airtight container.

VARIATION

Pinto beans are widely available, but if you cannot find them or you wish to vary the recipe, you can use cannellini beans or black-eyed beans as an alternative.

STEP 1

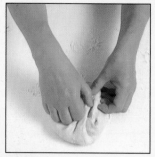

STEP 2

STEP 3

STEP 4

TORTILLAS

Tortillas are eaten with almost everything in Mexico in place of bread. Traditionally, tortillas are made with masa harina (coarse-textured maize meal) but they can also be made with wheat flour. A mixture of maize meal and all-purpose flour also makes an excellent tortilla.

MAKES 10

WHEAT TORTILLAS:
2¹/₂ cups all-purpose white flour
1 tsp salt
¹/₄ cup white vegetable shortening
²/₃–³/₄ cup warm water

CORN TORTILLAS:
1¹/₄ cups all-purpose white flour
1 tsp salt
1¹/₄ cups maize meal
3 tbsp white vegetable shortening
²/₃–³/₄ cup warm water

1 To make the wheat tortillas, sift the flour and salt into a bowl, and rub the fat into the flour with your fingertips until the mixture resembles very fine bread crumbs.

2 Add sufficient warm water to mix to a softish pliable dough; transfer to a lightly floured counter, and knead until smooth (2–3 minutes). Place in a plastic bag and let sit for about 15 minutes. (Steps 1 and 2 may be done in a food processor.)

3 Divide the dough into 10 equal pieces, and keep covered with a damp cloth to prevent it from drying out.

Roll out each piece of dough on a lightly floured counter to a circle of 7–8 inches. Place between paper towels as they are made, to prevent them from drying out.

4 Heat a griddle or heavy-based skillet until just beginning to smoke. Do not grease the pan. Brush off all excess flour from each tortilla. Place in the pan, and cook for 20–30 seconds only on each side until just speckled brown. They will quickly bubble from the heat, and should be pressed down lightly with a spatula occasionally during cooking. Take care not to burn them. If black deposits appear in the pan, scrape them off; they are excess burnt flour from the tortillas.

5 Wrap the tortillas in a clean dish cloth or place between paper towels when cooked to keep them pliable. When cold, wrap in plastic wrap if they are not to be used at once. They will keep in the refrigerator for several days.

6 Corn tortillas are made in a similar way, except the flour and salt is sifted into a bowl, the maize meal is mixed in, and then the fat is rubbed in finely; then continue as for wheat tortillas.

NACHOS

These are triangles of tortilla, deep-fried until they are crisp, and topped with a variety of spicy mixtures and grated cheese to brown either under the broiler or in the oven.

STEP 1

MAKES 30

5 wheat or corn tortillas (see page 12)
oil for frying
1 red bell pepper, halved and deseeded
10 ounce jar tomato salsa dip
4 scallions, trimmed and chopped
4 tomatoes, peeled and chopped
1 pound can refried beans or 1 quantity
  Refried Beans (see page 22)
1½ cups grated sharp Cheddar cheese
3 tbsp grated Parmesan cheese
chopped fresh cilantro to garnish

1 Stack the tortillas neatly, cut in half with a sharp knife, and then cut each half into 3 wedges to give 6 nachos from each tortilla.

2 Heat about 1 in. of oil in a large skillet until just smoking. Fry the pieces of tortilla – a few at a time – until crispy and lightly browned, turning once. Remove and drain on paper towels before transferring to baking sheets.

3 Put the bell pepper, cut-side downwards, into a broiler pan and place under a preheated moderate broiler until the skin is charred. Remove and let cool slightly. Peel off the skin, and then chop the bell pepper.

4 Put the chopped bell pepper in a bowl with the salsa dip, scallions, and tomatoes, and mix well.

5 Mash the refried beans, and spread an even layer over each nacho. Top with the tomato salsa mixture.

6 Sprinkle with the cheeses, and place under a preheated moderate broiler until the cheese bubbles. Alternatively, place in a preheated oven at 400°F for about 10 minutes until the cheese is bubbling. Serve hot or cold, sprinkled with chopped cilantro.

STEP 2

SKINNING BELL PEPPERS

When you are grilling bell peppers in order to skin them, make sure the skin is burnt black or you will not be able to peel it off easily.

SERVING NACHOS

The choice of toppings for nachos is unlimited, and they may be served hot or cold as an appetizer, a snack, or an accompaniment for drinks.

STEP 5

STEP 6

STEP 1

STEP 2

STEP 3

STEP 4

GUACAMOLE

This classic Mexican avocado dip is served as an accompaniment to many other dishes as well as being enjoyed as an appetizer, served with tacos for scooping it up.

SERVES 4

4–6 scallions, trimmed
2 large ripe avocados, quartered, pitted, and
    peeled
1 tbsp lime juice
2–3 crushed garlic cloves
few drops of Tabasco sauce
2–4 tomatoes, peeled, deseeded, and finely
    chopped
1–2 tbsp sour cream (optional)
salt and pepper
1 tbsp chopped fresh cilantro or chives

1 Put the scallions into a food processor, and chop finely. Cut the avocado into slices. Add to the food processor, and work until smooth. Alternatively, chop the scallions finely with a knife, and mash the avocados and scallions together with a fork.

2 Add the lime juice, garlic, and Tabasco sauce to the avocado mixture, and work or mash until the mixture is smoothly blended. Transfer to a bowl.

3 Stir in the chopped tomatoes, and sour cream, if using, and season to taste. Then mix in half the chopped cilantro or chives.

4 Turn the guacamole into a serving bowl, and if it is not to be used immediately, bury one of the avocado pits in it, as this will help it to keep its color. Cover tightly with plastic wrap until you are ready to use it, removing the pit at the last minute, and sprinkling with the remaining cilantro or chives.

5 Serve as an appetizer with tacos or tortillas, or as an accompaniment to such dishes as Chili con Carne (see page 58) or Chili Lamb Chops (see page 54); or use with other ingredients as a topping for tortillas, or as part of other recipes.

HOT, HOT, HOT!

You can vary the chili content of guacamole to suit your taste by increasing the amount of Tabasco sauce.

MASHING AVOCADOS

If you are making guacamole without the aid of a food processor, use very ripe avocados, or they will not mash easily to give a creamy texture to the guacamole.

STEP 3

STEP 4

STEP 5

STEP 6

TOSTADOS

These small round tortillas are deep-fried and topped with refried beans, shredded lettuce, and either a fish or egg mixture. Garnish with tomatoes, olives, and a creamy avocado sauce and serve cold as a delicious appetizer or light snack.

MAKES 8

½ quantity wheat or corn tortilla recipe (see page 12)
oil for frying
1 pound can refried beans, mashed or 1 quantity Refried Beans (see page 22)
finely shredded lettuce
7 ounce can shrimp or tuna fish in brine, well drained, or 4–6 hard-cooked eggs, coarsely grated
2–3 tsp sweet chili sauce
¼ tsp ground cumin
5–6 tbsp sour cream
3 tomatoes, sliced
2 small ripe avocados
3–4 scallions, trimmed and sliced
1–2 crushed garlic cloves
1 tbsp lime juice
salt and pepper

TO GARNISH:
pitted black olives, halved
fresh cilantro or parsley

1 Make up the tortilla recipe and divide into 8 even-sized pieces, keeping them covered with a damp cloth. Roll out each piece to a thin circle of about 5 inches on a lightly floured counter. Cook in the same manner as for large tortillas.

2 Heat about 1 in. of oil in a large skillet, and when just smoking, fry the tortillas, one at a time, for about a minute until they are a pale golden-brown on each side and just crispy. Drain on paper towels, and let cool.

3 Mash the refried beans, and spread a layer over each tortilla. Sprinkle with shredded lettuce.

4 Combine the drained shrimp or tuna fish (mashing them if necessary), or eggs, chili sauce, cumin, and sour cream, and place a spoonful to one side of each tortilla on the lettuce. Arrange the tomato slices down the other side.

5 Mash the avocados thoroughly with the scallions, garlic, and lime juice, or process in a food processor until smooth. Season to taste. Place a spoonful of the avocado sauce on top of the other ingredients.

6 Garnish each with halved and pitted black olives and cilantro leaves or parsley sprigs. Serve within an hour of preparing, or the tortilla may become soggy and the avocado will lose its color.

CHAPTER TWO

Vegetables & Salads

The excellent fruit and vegetables that appear in colorful profusion in the Mexican market places can be incorporated into delicious dishes to make vegetarian meals, attractive salads, and a range of accompaniments. These dishes use a combination of ingredients that may sound a little unusual but produce wonderful results.

Dried beans are an important part of the Mexican diet and feature in many dishes; one of the favorite types is the pink pinto bean, although black beans, red kidney beans, and garbanzo beans are popular too. They need long, slow cooking to tenderize and to absorb the rich and spicy flavors that are added, but salt should never be added before they are tender or they may never become really edible. Pre-soaking helps to reduce the cooking time, but there is no short cut to producing the best stewed beans – only time. When cooked, they can be cooked again to make Refried Beans, a dish that can be eaten on its own or as an ingredient in many other dishes.

Probably the most popular of all Mexican salads is Tomato Salsa. It has many variations, and each family has its own special method of preparation, but however it is served, it invariably includes sliced juicy red tomatoes, mixed with sliced or chopped red onions, chilis, and lime juice.

Opposite: *A giant desert cactus thrives in Mexico's arid scrub land.*

STEP 2

STEP 3

STEP 5

STEP 6

BASIC STEWED BEANS

Basic stewed beans are used in a variety of Mexican recipes. The cooking time depends on the type and age of the beans – anything between 1½ and 3 hours. Once cooked, they can be used in other recipes. Don't add salt until the beans are tender – it prevents them from softening.

SERVES 4

1¼ cups pinto beans or cannellini beans
1 large onion, sliced
2 garlic cloves, crushed
4 cups water
salt
chopped fresh cilantro or parsley to garnish

BEAN STEW:
1 large onion, sliced
2 garlic cloves, crushed
8 slices bacon, rinded and diced
2 tbsp oil
14 ounce can chopped tomatoes
1 tsp ground cumin
1 tsp sweet chili sauce

REFRIED BEANS:
1 onion, chopped
2 crushed garlic cloves
2 tbsp oil

1 Soak the beans in cold water overnight; or if time is short, cover the beans with boiling water, and leave until cold – about 2 hours.

2 Drain the beans, and put into a saucepan with the onion, garlic, and water. Bring to a boil, cover and simmer gently for 1½ hours. Stir well, add more boiling water if necessary, and simmer, covered, for a further 30–90 minutes, or until the beans are tender.

3 When the beans are tender, add salt to taste (about 1 teaspoon), and continue to cook, uncovered, for about 15 minutes to let most of the liquor evaporate to form a thick sauce.

4 Serve the basic beans hot, sprinkled with chopped cilantro; or cool, chill and reheat to serve next day; or use in another dish.

5 To make a bean stew, fry the onion, garlic, and bacon for 3–4 minutes in the oil. Add the canned tomatoes, the basic beans, cumin, and chili sauce, and bring to a boil. Cover and simmer very gently for 30 minutes. Adjust the seasoning, and serve.

6 To make refried beans, fry the onion and garlic in the oil until golden-brown. Then add a quarter of the basic beans with a little of their liquor, and mash. Continue adding and mashing the beans, while simmering over a low heat until thick. Adjust the seasoning, and serve hot; alternatively, cool and chill for up to 1 week.

STEP 1

STEP 2

STEP 3

STEP 4

TOMATO SALSA

This salad is used extensively in Mexican cooking as anything from a dip to a relish, and makes its appearance on the table as an accompaniment to almost any dish.

SERVES 4

4 ripe red tomatoes
1 medium red-skinned onion or 6 scallions
1–2 garlic cloves, crushed (optional)
2 tbsp chopped fresh cilantro
$\frac{1}{2}$ red or green chili (optional)
finely grated rind of $\frac{1}{2}$–1 lemon or lime
1–2 tbsp lemon or lime juice
pepper

1 Chop the tomatoes fairly finely and evenly, and put into a bowl. They must be firm and a good strong red color for the best results, but if preferred, they may be peeled by placing them in boiling water for about 20 seconds, and then plunging into cold water. The skins should then slip off easily when nicked with a knife.

2 Peel and slice the red onions thinly, or trim the scallions, and cut into thin slanting slices. Add to the tomatoes with the garlic and cilantro, and mix together lightly.

3 Remove the seeds from the red or green chili, chop the flesh very finely, and add to the salad. Treat the chilis with care; wash your hands thoroughly after handling them.

4 Add the lemon or lime rind and juice, and mix well. Transfer to a serving bowl and sprinkle with pepper.

USING CHILIS

Take care when chopping chilis as they can burn your skin. Handle them as little as possible – you could even wear rubber gloves if you wish. Always wash your hands thoroughly afterward, and don't touch your face or eyes before you have washed your hands. Remove chili seeds before chopping the chilis, as they are the hottest part, and shouldn't be allowed to slip into the food.

VARIATION

If you don't like the distinctive flavor of fresh cilantro, you can replace it with Italian parsley instead.

STORING

Tomato salsa may be covered with plastic wrap and stored in the refrigerator for up to 36 hours before use.

MEXICAN RICE

This is a traditional way of cooking rice in Mexico. Onions, garlic, tomatoes, chilis, and vegetables are added to the rice and cooked in a chicken or vegetable stock.

STEP 2

SERVES 6

scant 1 1/2 cups long-grain rice
3 tbsp oil
1 large onion, chopped
1/2 chili, deseeded and chopped finely (see page 24)
2 large garlic cloves, crushed
4 tomatoes (about 8 ounces), peeled and chopped
1 cup carrots, peeled and chopped
3 1/2 cups chicken or vegetable stock
3/4 cup frozen peas (optional)
salt and pepper
chopped fresh cilantro or parsley to garnish

1 Put the rice in a heatproof bowl, cover with boiling water and let sit for 10 minutes, then drain it very thoroughly.

2 Heat the oil in a pan. Add the rice and fry over a low heat, stirring almost constantly for about 5 minutes, or until just beginning to color.

3 Add the chopped onion, chili, garlic, tomatoes, and carrots to the pan, and continue to cook for a minute or so before adding the stock and bringing to a boil.

4 Stir the rice well, cover the pan and simmer over a low heat for 20 minutes without removing the lid.

5 Stir in the peas, if using, and seasoning. Continue to cook, covered, for about 5 minutes, or until all the liquid has been absorbed, and the rice is tender.

6 If time allows, let the covered pan sit for 5–10 minutes, and then fork up the rice. Sprinkle generously with either chopped fresh cilantro or parsley before serving.

STEP 3

STEP 5

ADDING CHILIS

The chili content of this dish can be increased to give a hotter "Mexican" taste, but be warned – once it has been added, it cannot be removed!

STEP 6

STEP 1

STEP 1

STEP 4

STEP 5

CHRISTMAS SALAD

This colorful salad is served as an accompaniment, but could easily be served as a main dish. It incorporates vegetables, fruits, and nuts to give a wide variety of flavors and textures. It is usually served around Christmas time in Mexico.

SERVES 4

1 romaine lettuce
4 ounces cooked beets
2 oranges
1 green-skinned eating apple
1–2 bananas
1 tbsp lime or lemon juice
1 carrot, peeled
1 pomegranate or paw-paw
$^{1}/_{2}$ cup roasted peanuts or slivered almonds, toasted

DRESSING:
1 tbsp lime or lemon juice
finely grated rind of $^{1}/_{4}$ lime or lemon
   (optional)
1 garlic clove, crushed
4 tbsp light olive oil or sunflower oil
1 tsp sugar
salt and pepper

1 Shred the lettuce, and arrange on a flat dish. Peel the beet if necessary, and cut into dice or small slices; then arrange around the edge of the lettuce.

2 Cut away the peel and pith from the oranges, and ease out the segments carefully from between the membranes. Arrange the orange segments over the lettuce.

3 Core and chop the apple, and put into a bowl with the sliced bananas. Add the lime or lemon juice, and toss; then drain off the excess juice.

4 Cut the carrot into julienne strips, or peel off in thin strips, using a potato peeler. Add to the apple mixture and spoon over the salad.

5 Cut the pomegranate into quarters and ease out the seeds, or halve the paw-paw, discard the seeds, and peel and dice the flesh. Sprinkle over the salad with the peanuts or almonds.

6 Whisk together all the ingredients for the dressing and either spoon over the salad or serve in a jug.

ADVANCE PREPARATION

The salad may be prepared up to 1 hour ahead, but without adding the dressing. Cover with plastic wrap and chill until required. If left any longer, the beet will probably bleed into the other ingredients, and spoil the appearance.

MEXICAN SALAD

Cooked new potatoes and blanched cauliflower are combined with carrots, olives, capers, and gherkins in a tangy mustard dressing for a salad suitable as an accompaniment or as a main dish.

STEP 3

STEP 4

STEP 5

STEP 6

SERVES 4

1 pound small new potatoes, scraped
salt
8 ounces small cauliflower florets
1–2 carrots, peeled
3 large gherkins
2–3 scallions, trimmed
1–2 tbsp capers
12 pitted black olives
1 iceberg lettuce or other lettuce leaves

DRESSING:
1½–2 tsp Dijon mustard
1 tsp sugar
2 tbsp olive oil
4 tbsp thick mayonnaise
1 tbsp wine vinegar
salt and pepper

TO GARNISH:
1 ripe avocado
1 tbsp lime or lemon juice

1 Cook the potatoes in salted water until they are just tender; drain, cool, and either dice or slice. Cook the cauliflower in boiling salted water for 2 minutes. Drain, rinse under cold water, and drain again.

2 Cut the carrots into narrow julienne strips and mix with the potatoes and cauliflower.

3 Cut the gherkins and scallions into slanting slices, and add to the salad with the capers and black olives.

4 Arrange the lettuce leaves on a plate or in a bowl, and spoon the salad over the lettuce.

5 To make the dressing, whisk all the ingredients together until completely emulsified and season to taste. Drizzle over the salad.

6 Cut the avocado into quarters, remove the pit, and peel. Cut into slices, and dip immediately in the lime or lemon juice. Use to garnish the salad just before serving.

USING DIFFERENT VEGETABLES

This salad is a very versatile one – you can incorporate or substitute a variety of other vegetables, such as cabbage, peas, or zucchini, according to your own personal preferences.

CHAPTER THREE

Light Meals & Snacks

Tortillas are one of the staple foods of Mexico. They can be shaped, rolled, cut, fried, layered, baked, and prepared in numerous other ways to give the widest possible variety of snacks. They can be served hot and cold, eaten in your fingers or with a fork, and can be dressed up with countless flavorings, both savory and sweet. The words Tacos, Quesadillas, Burritos, and Fajitas all evoke wonderful pictures of Mexican life; their spicy flavors, with a touch of Spanish here and Indian there, are equally distinctive. Mexico has a hot climate and the food tends to be hot and spicy, but the heat of the food often seems to counteract the heat of the sun.

Tempting snacks such as the ones in this section are sold in market places to Mexicans and visitors alike. They are simple to make, for very few Mexican dishes are complicated, just very tasty – so be adventurous and serve them to your family and friends at home.

Opposite: *Fresh tortilla snacks being cooked and sold in a market in Mexico City.*

STEP 1

STEP 2

STEP 4

STEP 5

MEXICAN TACOS

One of the classic Mexican dishes, which everyone knows. Either prepare your own taco shells or buy them ready-made, and fill with refried beans, spicy ground beef, shredded lettuce, and sour cream to serve with tomato salsa and guacamole.

SERVES 4

1½ cups lean ground beef
1 onion, chopped finely
3 garlic cloves, crushed
1 chili, deseeded and very finely chopped (see page 24)
1 celery stalk, finely chopped
1 red bell pepper
3 tomatoes, peeled and chopped
1 tbsp tomato paste
½ tsp ground cumin
½ tsp ground cinnamon
salt and pepper
1 tbsp vinegar
2 tbsp stock or water
1 tbsp chopped fresh cilantro (optional)
oil for frying
4 wheat or corn tortillas (see page 12)

TO SERVE:
1 pound can refried beans
shredded lettuce
4 tbsp sour cream
Guacamole (see page 16)
Tomato Salsa (see page 24)

1 Put the beef into a pan with the onion, garlic, chili, and celery, and cook over a low heat, stirring frequently, for 10 minutes or until cooked through.

2 Cut the bell pepper in half, remove the seeds and place in the broiler pan, cut-side down. Place under a preheated moderate broiler until charred. Let cool slightly, then peel off the skin, and chop the bell pepper.

3 Add the bell pepper and tomatoes to the beef mixture, followed by the tomato paste, spices, seasoning, vinegar, and stock. Simmer for 10 minutes, until tender, and all the liquid has evaporated. Stir in the cilantro, if using.

4 If making your own taco shells, heat about 1 in. of oil in a skillet, and when just smoking, add a tortilla, and fry briefly until just beginning to color, folding in half during cooking. Remove quickly and drain on paper towels, placing crumpled paper towels in the center of the taco so it sets in a shell shape. If using bought taco shells, warm gently in the oven.

5 Mash the refried beans, and put a layer in the base of each taco; then cover with the beef mixture, dividing it equally between each taco. Sprinkle with shredded lettuce and drizzle with sour cream. Serve on warmed plates with guacamole and tomato salsa.

STEP 1

STEP 2

STEP 4

STEP 4

QUESADILLAS

These are an ideal vegetarian dish. A "lightly hot" flavoring is given to the mixture of cheeses, scallions, and cilantro that makes up the filling for these folded tortillas, which are baked in the oven.

SERVES 4

8 corn or wheat tortillas (see page 12)

FILLING:
6 ounces Feta cheese or white Cheshire cheese
6 ounces Mozzarella cheese
6 tbsp grated Parmesan cheese
6 scallions, trimmed and chopped
1–2 garlic cloves, crushed
1 tbsp sweet chili sauce
1 tbsp chopped fresh cilantro
1 cooked potato, coarsely grated
salt and pepper
beaten egg or egg white
oil for brushing

TO SERVE:
shredded lettuce
Tomato Salsa (see page 24)

1 To make the filling, grate the Feta and Mozzarella cheeses coarsely into a bowl, and mix in the Parmesan cheese, scallions, garlic, chili sauce, cilantro, potato, and seasoning.

2 If the tortillas are too firm to bend in half, dip each one into a pan of gently simmering water until just soft, and drain on paper towels.

3 Place about 1½ tablespoons of the cheese filling on one side of each tortilla, and fold in half.

4 Brush the edges with beaten egg or egg white. Fold over, and press the edges together well.

5 Place the quesadillas on lightly greased baking sheets, and brush each with a little oil. Cook in a preheated oven at 375°F for 12–15 minutes until lightly browned.

6 Serve the quesadillas either hot or warm with shredded lettuce and tomato salsa as accompaniments.

ALTERNATIVE FILLINGS

This cheese filling makes Quesadillas an excellent dish for vegetarians, but the filling can equally well be based on fish or meat instead. Eggs are another tasty choice for vegetarians.

PORK TACOS

A different way of serving tacos – here the tortillas are rolled with the spicy pork filling inside, and then fried to give a crispy outer shell. They may be served with guacamole, tomato salsa, and sour cream, and can be served cold.

STEP 1

MAKES 8

oil for frying
1½ cups lean ground pork
2 slices bacon, derinded and chopped
1 onion, very finely chopped
2 garlic cloves, crushed
1 tbsp sweet chili sauce
1–2 tbsp tomato paste
½ tsp ground cumin
½ tsp dried oregano
salt and pepper
⅓ cup chopped button mushrooms
2 tbsp stock or water
8 wheat or corn tortillas (see page 12)
salad greens to garnish

1 Heat the oil in a saucepan, add the ground pork, bacon, onion, and garlic, and cook over a low heat, stirring frequently, for about 10 minutes, until almost cooked.

2 Add the chili sauce, tomato paste, cumin, oregano, and seasoning, and continue to cook for a few minutes more; then add the mushrooms and stock or water, and cook for a further 2–3 minutes. Adjust the seasoning, and let cool.

3 Divide the pork mixture between the tortillas. Fold in the ends, and roll them up tightly; then secure each one with a wooden toothpick to prevent unrolling while cooking.

4 Heat about 1 in. of oil in a large skillet and when just smoking, add the taco rolls, 2 at a time, and fry until a light golden-brown all over, turning in the oil as necessary. Alternatively, they may be cooked in deep fat at 350°F until a light golden-brown.

5 Drain the taco rolls thoroughly on paper towels and remove the toothpicks carefully. Keep warm while frying the remainder. Serve with a garnish of salad greens.

STEP 3

STEP 3

VARIATION

These tacos may be made with fillings based on fish, eggs, vegetables, and different types of meat. Experiment to find your own tasty recipe!

STEP 4

STEP 1

STEP 2

STEP 4

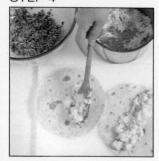

STEP 5

BURRITOS

A filling of scrambled eggs, together with a spicy pumpkin seed, herb and yogurt mixture, and sliced tomatoes, is rolled into either wheat or corn tortillas. Chopped ham, bacon, or fish can be added for variety.

SERVES 4

¹/₃ cup pumpkin seeds, toasted
3–4 scallions, trimmed and sliced
1 chili, deseeded and finely chopped (see page 24)
4 tbsp chopped fresh parsley
1 tbsp chopped fresh cilantro
6 tbsp natural yogurt
4 wheat or corn tortillas (see page 12)
2 tbsp butter
4 tbsp milk
1 garlic clove, crushed
salt and pepper
6 eggs
1¹/₄ cups chopped cooked ham or bacon, or 1¹/₂ cups flaked cooked white or smoked fish
2 tomatoes, peeled and sliced

TO GARNISH:
shredded lettuce
Tomato Salsa (see page 24)

1 Toast the pumpkin seeds lightly (under a moderate broiler or in a heavy-based skillet with no added fat), and then chop finely, or put into a food processor with the scallions and chili and work until well blended.

2 Add the parsley and cilantro, followed by the yogurt, and blend until well mixed. Season to taste.

3 Warm the tortillas, wrapped in foil, in a preheated oven at 350°F for a few minutes.

4 Melt the butter in a pan with the milk, garlic, and seasoning. Remove from the heat, and beat in the eggs. Cook over a low heat, stirring continuously, until just scrambled – do not overcook. Stir in the ham, bacon, or fish.

5 Lay out the tortillas, spoon the scrambled egg down the centre of each and top with the pumpkin seed mixture followed by the sliced tomatoes.

6 Roll up the tortillas, and serve as they are, garnished with the shredded lettuce and tomato salsa.

MICROWAVE HINT

If preferred, the burritos may be reheated before serving for 1 minute in a microwave oven set on Full Power.

STEP 1

STEP 2

STEP 3

STEP 5

CHICKEN FAJITAS

This spicy chicken filling, made up of mixed bell peppers, chilis, and mushrooms and flavored strongly with lime, is put into folded tortillas, and topped with sour cream to serve with tomato salsa. Many other fillings can be used to suit your taste: the possibilities are endless.

SERVES 4

2 red bell peppers
2 green bell peppers
2 tbsp olive oil
2 onions, chopped
3 garlic cloves, crushed
1 chili, deseeded and finely chopped (see
    page 24)
2 boneless chicken breasts (about
    12 ounces)
$1/3$ cup sliced button mushrooms
2 tsp chopped fresh cilantro
grated rind of $1/2$ lime
2 tbsp lime juice
4 wheat or corn tortillas (see page 12)
4–6 tbsp sour cream
salt and pepper

TO GARNISH:
Tomato Salsa (see page 24)
lime wedges

1 Cut the bell peppers in half, and remove the seeds. Place, skin-side upward, under a preheated moderate broiler until well charred. Let cool slightly, and then peel off the skin; cut into thin slices.

2 Heat the oil in a pan. Add the onions, garlic, and chili, and fry

them for a few minutes until the onion has softened.

3 Cut the chicken into narrow strips. Add to the vegetable mixture in the pan, and fry for 4–5 minutes until almost cooked through, stirring occasionally.

4 Add the bell peppers, mushrooms, cilantro, lime rind, and juice, and continue to cook for 2–3 minutes. Season to taste.

5 Heat the tortillas, wrapped in foil, in a preheated oven at 350°F for a few minutes. Bend each of the tortillas in half, and divide the chicken mixture between them.

6 Top the chicken filling in each tortilla with a spoonful of sour cream, and serve garnished with tomato salsa and lime wedges.

SEAFOOD ALTERNATIVE

Instead of chicken, 8–10 ounces of peeled shrimp or jumbo shrimp may be used to give a tasty seafood snack.

CHAPTER FOUR

Main Dishes

Fish and shellfish abound both in the bustling seafood markets of Mexico, and all along the coastline where the local fishermen sell their morning catch directly from their boats. Invariably, the seafood is cooked by the simplest of methods, often just with lime juice and with fresh vegetables, spices, and herbs, whether it is to be eaten at home with the family or in a restaurant. One specialty called ceviche, consisting of raw fillets of fish or shellfish, is very easy to prepare, as it is simply marinated liberally in lime juice, which gives it the appearance and taste of being cooked.

Chicken appears frequently on the menu, while turkey, duck, and game are often served on special occasions. All poultry and game dishes are cooked with robust flavorings of spices and herbs, and often incorporate fresh vegetables and fruits, which add both to the taste and texture.

All types of meat feature extensively in Mexican main dishes and appear in many guises, all with a deep, rich flavor. The sauces for all meat dishes tend to be fairly hot and spicy, usually with a liberal addition of fresh or dried chili or some type of chili sauce, but of course this can be adapted to suit your own particular taste – simply cut down on the amount of chili used in the recipe to give a milder but still spicy sauce.

Opposite: *The beach at Acapulco. Fish are plentiful off Mexico's coasts and are used in a variety of tasty dishes.*

STEP 1

STEP 2

STEP 3

STEP 4

BACON-WRAPPED SHRIMP WITH SOUR CREAM

Jumbo shrimp make a splendid meal, especially when wrapped in bacon, broiled with a garlic and lime butter, and served with a spicy and tangy sour cream and cilantro sauce.

SERVES 4

16–20 jumbo shrimp
16–20 lean slices bacon, derinded
¹/₄ cup butter
finely grated rind of 1 lime
2 garlic cloves, crushed

CILANTRO AND SOUR CREAM SAUCE:
²/₃ cup sour cream
2–3 garlic cloves, crushed
¹/₂ small red chili, deseeded and very finely
 chopped (see page 24)
2 tbsp chopped fresh cilantro
2 scallions, trimmed and finely chopped
salt and pepper
1–2 tsp lime juice

TO GARNISH:
fresh cilantro
lime wedges

1 Remove the heads and shells from the shrimp, but leave the tails in place. Remove the black vein which runs down the length of the shrimp.

2 Wrap a slice of bacon around each shrimp, securing with a piece of wooden toothpick. Place on a foil-lined broiler pan.

3 Melt the butter, and mix in half the grated lime rind and the garlic. Use to brush over the bacon-wrapped shrimp.

4 To make the sauce, put the soured cream into a bowl, and mix in the garlic, chili, cilantro, scallions, remaining grated lime rind, seasoning, and finally lime juice to taste, which will thicken up the sauce. Transfer to a serving bowl.

5 Cook the shrimp under a preheated broiler for about 2 minutes on each side, or until the bacon is lightly browned and the shrimp hot. Remove and discard the wooden toothpicks.

6 Serve the shrimp on a large plate or 4 individual plates, together with the sauce, and a garnish of fresh cilantro and lime wedges.

COOKING SHRIMP

If you buy raw shrimp to use in this recipe, cook them first briefly in boiling water until they turn pink.

46

YUCATAN FISH

Herbs, onion, green bell pepper, and pumpkin seeds are used to flavor this baked fish dish, which is first marinated in lime juice.

STEP 1

STEP 2

STEP 4

STEP 5

SERVES 4

4 cod cutlets or steaks or hake cutlets (about 6 ounces each)
2 tbsp lime juice
salt and pepper
1 green bell pepper
1 tbsp olive oil
1 onion, chopped finely
1–2 garlic cloves, crushed
$^1/_3$ cup green pumpkin seeds
grated rind of $^1/_2$ lime
1 tbsp chopped fresh cilantro or parsley
1 tbsp chopped fresh mixed herbs
$^1/_2$ cup thinly sliced button mushrooms
2–3 tbsp fresh orange juice or white wine

TO GARNISH:
lime wedges
fresh mixed herbs

1 Wipe the fish, and place in a shallow ovenproof dish. Pour the lime juice over, and turn the fish in the juice. Season with salt and pepper. Cover and leave in a cool place for 15–30 minutes.

2 Halve the bell pepper, and remove the seeds. Place under a preheated moderate broiler, skin-side upward, until it burns and splits. Let cool slightly, then peel off the skin, and chop the flesh.

3 Heat the oil in a pan, and fry the onion, garlic, bell pepper, and pumpkin seeds over a low heat for a few minutes until the onion is soft.

4 Stir in the lime rind, cilantro, mixed herbs, mushrooms, and seasoning, and spoon over the fish.

5 Spoon or pour the orange juice or wine over the fish. Cover with foil or a lid, and place in a preheated oven at 350°F for about 30 minutes, or until the fish is just tender.

6 Garnish the fish with lime wedges and fresh herbs, and serve with Mexican Rice (see page 27) or plain boiled rice and tortillas.

MICROWAVE NOTE

This dish may also be covered with plastic wrap, and cooked in a microwave oven at Full Power for about 4 minutes.

ENCHILADA LAYERS

The filling for these can be varied considerably by using beef, fish, or shellfish. If preferred, the tortillas can be rolled up after they are filled, and baked in the sauce in rolls rather than in layers.

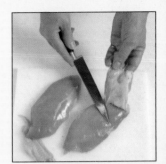

STEP 1

STEP 2

STEP 5

STEP 5

SERVES 4

CHICKEN FILLING:
1 pound boneless chicken breasts
2 tbsp olive oil
1 large onion, thinly sliced
3 garlic cloves, crushed
1 tsp ground cumin
2 tbsp stock or water
1 tbsp chopped fresh cilantro
salt and pepper
chopped fresh cilantro to garnish

TOMATO SAUCE:
2 tbsp oil
1 onion, very finely chopped
3 garlic cloves, crushed
1 red chili, deseeded and finely chopped
    (see page 24)
14 ounce can chopped tomatoes with
    herbs
8 ounce can peeled tomatoes, chopped
3 tbsp tomato paste
2 tbsp lime juice
2 tsp superfine sugar
6 wheat or corn tortillas (see page 12)
1½ cups coarsely grated Feta or white
    Cheshire cheese

1 Remove the skin from the chicken breasts and chop the flesh finely. Heat the oil in a pan, and fry the onion and garlic over a low heat until the onion has softened.

2 Add the chicken, and fry for about 5 minutes, or until well sealed and almost cooked, stirring frequently. Add the cumin, stock or water, and seasoning, and continue to cook for 2–3 minutes until tender; then stir in the cilantro, and remove from the heat.

3 To make the tomato sauce, heat the oil in a pan, and fry the onion, garlic, and chili gently until softened.

4 Add both cans of tomatoes, the tomato paste, lime juice, sugar, and seasoning. Bring to a boil and simmer over a low heat for 10 minutes.

5 Place 1 tortilla on a greased ovenproof dish, cover with a fifth of the chicken mixture and 2 tablespoons of tomato sauce, and sprinkle with cheese. Continue to layer like this, finishing with a tortilla, the remaining sauce, and cheese.

6 Place, uncovered, in a preheated oven at 375°F for about 25 minutes, or until lightly browned on top. Serve cut into wedges, and sprinkle with chopped cilantro.

PICADILLO

This spicy meat hash can be made with beef or with a mixture of beef and pork. It is flavored with plenty of spices, chili, raisins, and almonds, and may be used as it is, or as a filling for tortillas (see page 12), burritos (see page 40), enchiladas (see page 51), taco shells (see page 34), or chimichangas (see page 66).

STEP 1

STEP 2

STEP 3

STEP 3

SERVES 4

3 cups lean ground beef
2 cups ground pork (or beef)
2 onions, thinly sliced
3 garlic cloves, crushed
1 large carrot, finely chopped
1 green chili, deseeded and finely chopped
  (see page 24)
14 ounce can tomatoes
2 tbsp tomato paste
$^1/_2$ cup raisins
$^2/_3$ cup red wine
1 tbsp vinegar
1 tsp cumin
$^1/_2$ tsp ground allspice
$^1/_2$ tsp ground cinnamon
$^1/_2$ cup blanched slivered almonds
salt and pepper
chopped fresh cilantro to garnish

1 Put the meat into a heavy-bottomed saucepan with no extra fat and cook over a low heat until well sealed, stirring frequently.

2 Add the onions, garlic, carrot, and chili, and continue to cook for 3–4 minutes, or until soft. Drain off any excess fat.

3 Add the tomatoes, tomato paste, raisins, wine, vinegar, cumin, allspice, cinnamon, half the slivered almonds, and seasoning. Stir into the meat and onion mixture.

4 Bring to a boil, cover the pan and simmer over a low heat, stirring occasionally, for 20–30 minutes, or until the meat is tender and most of the liquid has evaporated.

5 Adjust the seasoning to taste, and serve the picadillo sprinkled with the remaining slivered almonds and chopped cilantro.

STUFFING FOR VEGETABLES

This versatile recipe is excellent when topped with a layer of creamed potatoes. Alternatively, it can be used as a stuffing for bell peppers, zucchini, eggplants, and other vegetables.

CHILI LAMB CHOPS

Leg lamb chops, cut straight across the leg, make a very tender and tasty meal when given the Mexican flavoring of chili, onion, spices, and lime.

STEP 1

STEP 3

STEP 5

STEP 6

SERVES 4

4 large lamb leg chops (about 6 ounces each)
²/₃ cup red wine
3 large garlic cloves, crushed
¹/₂ small onion, chopped
1 small chili, deseeded and finely chopped
   (see page 24)
2 small thin slices fresh root ginger, chopped
1 tbsp paprika
1¹/₂ tsp ground cumin
¹/₂ tsp salt
pepper
grated rind of ¹/₂ lime
2 tbsp lime juice
oil for frying

TO GARNISH:
lime slices, twisted
2 scallions, trimmed and sliced
chopped fresh cilantro or cilantro leaves

1 Cover the lamb chops with plastic wrap, and beat out a little thinner with a meat cleaver or rolling pin.

2 Put the wine into a food processor or blender with the garlic, onion, chili, ginger, paprika, cumin, salt, pepper, and lime rind, and juice, and work until smooth. Alternatively, chop the onion, chili, and garlic very finely,

and mix them thoroughly with the other ingredients.

3 Pour a thin layer of the sauce into a container just large enough to hold the lamb in a single layer. Add the lamb and cover with the remaining sauce.

4 Cover the lamb with plastic wrap and leave in a cool place to marinate for at least 2 hours, preferably 3–4 hours.

5 Heat the oil in a pan. Drain the pieces of lamb, and fry each one over a low heat for 3–4 minutes on each side until browned and just cooked through. Pour off any excess fat from the pan. Add the remaining marinade, and cook for 3–4 minutes. Adjust the seasoning.

6 Serve the lamb chops on a platter with the sauce spooned over and garnished with twisted lime slices, sliced scallions, and chopped fresh cilantro or cilantro leaves. Serve with fried or boiled potatoes, tortillas, and a salad.

SPICED PORK RIBS WITH APRICOTS

Pork ribs are baked with a selection of spices and then, halfway through cooking, a spicy apricot and onion sauce is added to produce a thick and delicious coating to the pork.

STEP 1

SERVES 4

3¹/₂–4 pounds pork ribs
salt
1 tbsp coarsely ground black pepper
1 tbsp ground cumin
4 garlic cloves, crushed
2 tbsp chopped fresh cilantro
1 tsp ground coriander
1 tbsp oil
chopped fresh cilantro to garnish (optional)

APRICOT SAUCE:
scant 2 cups chicken or beef stock
1 cup ready-to-eat dried apricot halves
4 garlic cloves, crushed
1 tbsp hot chili sauce or
  ¹/₂–1 tsp chili powder
2 tbsp oil
1 large onion, chopped

1 Cut the pork into pieces about 2 inches square and place in an ovenproof dish or pan in a single layer. Season with salt and pepper. Combine the cumin, garlic, fresh cilantro, and ground coriander, and sprinkle over the pork, rubbing in and turning the pieces so they are evenly coated. Let marinate for at least 2 hours.

2 Drizzle the oil over the pork, and place in a preheated oven at 400°F for 45 minutes, or until lightly browned.

3 Meanwhile, prepare the sauce. Put the stock, apricots, garlic, and chili sauce or powder into a food processor or blender, and work until puréed. Alternatively, chop finely and mix well.

4 Heat the 2 tablespoons of oil. Fry the onion until softened but only lightly colored. Add the apricot purée, bring to a boil, and simmer over a low heat for 10 minutes. (If necessary you can add a little hot water, but the sauce should be thick.)

5 Drain off any excess fat from the pork. Pour the apricot sauce over the ribs, and return to the oven for about 20 minutes, or until well browned. Serve hot sprinkled with chopped cilantro, if liked, and with a salad.

STEP 3

ALTERNATIVE

Alternatively, fry the pork in shallow fat until well browned and cooked through, then serve with the sauce spooned over.

STEP 4

STEP 5

STEP 1

STEP 2

STEP 3

STEP 4

CHILI CON CARNE

Probably the best-known Mexican dish and one that is a great favorite with all. The chili content can be increased to suit your taste.

SERVES 4

1½ pounds braising or best stewing steak
2 tbsp oil
1 large onion, sliced
2–4 garlic cloves, crushed
1 tbsp all-purpose flour
scant 2 cups tomato juice
14 ounce can tomatoes
1–2 tbsp sweet chili sauce
1 tsp ground cumin
salt and pepper
14 ounce can red kidney beans, drained
½ tsp dried oregano
1–2 tbsp chopped fresh parsley
chopped fresh herbs to garnish

1 Cut the beef into cubes of about ¾ in. Heat the oil in a flameproof casserole, and fry the beef until well sealed all over. Remove from the casserole.

2 Add the onion and garlic to the casserole, and fry in the same oil until lightly browned. Stir in the flour, and cook for 1–2 minutes.

3 Stir in the tomato juice and tomatoes gradually, and bring to a boil. Replace the beef, and add the chili sauce, cumin, and seasoning. Cover and

place in a preheated oven at 325°F for 1½ hours, or until almost tender.

4 Stir in the kidney beans, oregano, and parsley, and adjust the seasoning. Cover the casserole, and return to the oven for 45 minutes, or until the meat is very tender and the sauce is fairly thick.

5 Serve the chili con carne sprinkled with freshly chopped herbs and with boiled rice and tortillas.

GROUND BEEF

Traditionally, this dish is made with cubed beef, though ground beef is often used instead.

ECONOMY HINT

Because chili con carne requires quite a lengthy cooking time, it saves time and fuel to prepare double the quantity you need and freeze half of it to serve on another occasion. Defrost and use within 3–4 weeks.

CHILI MEATBALLS

Meatballs are a great favorite, and here both the meat and the tomato sauce are spiced, but the result is not too hot. By roasting the bell pepper and peeling off the skin, any bitterness is removed.

STEP 1

STEP 2

STEP 3

STEP 4

SERVES 4

1½ pounds ground beef
1 small onion, chopped finely
¼ cup ground almonds
1 cup fresh white bread crumbs
1 tsp ground cumin
¼ tsp mild chili powder
1 tsp chopped fresh thyme or ½ tsp dried thyme
salt and pepper
1 egg, beaten
3–4 tbsp oil for frying
sprigs of fresh thyme or parsley to garnish

SAUCE:
1 onion, sliced
8 ounces tomatoes, peeled
2 crushed garlic cloves
1¼ cups tomato juice
½–1 red chili, deseeded and finely chopped (see page 24)
1 tsp sweet chili sauce
1 red bell pepper

1 To make the meatballs, combine the beef, onion, ground almonds, bread crumbs, cumin, chili powder, herbs, and seasoning, and bind together with the beaten egg.

2 Divide into 16–20 pieces, and shape into round balls.

3 Heat the oil in a pan, and fry the meatballs until lightly browned; transfer to a casserole.

4 Purée the onion, tomatoes, and garlic in a food processor or blender, or chop finely and mix well. Pour into a saucepan with the tomato juice, chili, chili sauce, and seasoning. Bring to a boil, and simmer gently for 10 minutes.

5 Halve the bell pepper, and remove the seeds. Place under a preheated moderate broiler, skin-side upward, and cook until the skin chars. Let cool slightly, then peel off the skin, and cut the bell pepper into strips.

6 Add the bell pepper to the sauce, and pour over the meatballs. Cover the casserole, and place in a preheated oven at 325°F for 30–40 minutes.

7 Adjust the seasoning, and serve garnished with thyme or parsley. Serve with rice or potatoes and a salad.

CHAPTER FIVE

Desserts & Cakes

Many tropical fruits grow abundantly in Mexico, including pineapples, guavas, mangoes, passion-fruit, coconuts, and all the citrus fruits, and these are used in many of the desserts that are served. Mexicans also love fried pastries, fritters, and pieces of tortilla, which are tossed in a spicy sugar mixture after they are fried, and served hot or cold as a dessert or sweet snack.

Every country serves some type of ice cream and Mexico is no exception. Probably the favorite is either a vanilla ice cream with undertones of cinnamon and spices – delicious served alone or with fresh fruits – or a citrus ice cream made simply by adding finely grated lime, orange, or lemon rind to the mixture.

The Mexican version of Bread Pudding is fairly unusual but is certainly one that will quickly become a favorite. The bread is soaked in a spicy sugar syrup, together with raisins, nuts, and a thick grating of a sharp Cheddar cheese, then everything is wrapped in tortillas before baking – it is just as good cold as hot.

Yeasted buns and cakes are also popular, often with raisins and nuts added and always spiced in some way. These, along with other cakes, breads, and cookies, appear in various forms, often made to be served at the religious festivals held throughout the year.

Opposite: *The old Mayan Temple of the Dwarf at Uxmal, Yucatan.*

SWEET TORTILLA FRITTERS

Sweet tortillas are cut into triangles to be fried, and are served dipped in cinnamon sugar as teatime treats, or with fresh fruits and cream or yogurt for a dessert.

STEP 1

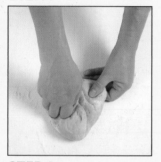

STEP 3

STEP 4

STEP 5

SERVES 4–6

2 eggs
3 tbsp superfine sugar
1 cup all-purpose flour
³/₄ cup self-rising flour
pinch of salt
¹/₄ tsp ground cinnamon
oil for shallow frying

CINNAMON SUGAR:
¹/₃ cup superfine sugar
¹/₂ tsp ground cinnamon
good pinch of ground ginger

TO DECORATE:
clear honey (optional)
mixed fresh fruits

1 Put the eggs and sugar into a bowl, and whisk together until very thick and pale in color, with the whisk leaving a distinct trail. It is best to use an electric hand mixer, if you have one.

2 Sift the two flours together with the salt and ground cinnamon. Whisk half of the flour gradually into the egg mixture, then work in the remainder to make a dough.

3 Transfer the dough to a lightly floured counter, and knead until smooth and no longer sticky. (This may be done in a large electric mixer fitted with a dough hook.) Wrap in plastic wrap, and let sit for about 30 minutes.

4 Divide the dough into 6, and roll each piece out to a thin circle of about 8 inches; then cut each circle into quarters.

5 Heat about 1 in. of oil in a pan until a cube of bread will brown in about 1 minute. Fry the fritters, a few at a time, for about a minute on each side, until golden brown and bubbly. Drain the fritters on paper towels, and toss quickly in a mixture of the sugar, cinnamon, and ginger.

6 Serve the fritters (hot or cold) on a plate, and, if liked, drizzle a little clear honey over them. Decorate with fresh fruits such as sliced mango, figs, passion-fruit, nectarines, peaches, strawberries, guavas, and pomegranates.

STEP 1

STEP 2

STEP 3

STEP 3

FRUIT CHIMICHANGAS

Wheat tortillas are folded into quarters with a filling of fruits such as paw-paw, guava, or mango, mixed with orange rind and orange segments and flavored with cinnamon and sugar, then fried in butter to make a truly delicious dessert.

SERVES 4

1 large paw-paw, or 2 guavas, or 1 large mango
8–12 strawberries
1 large orange
2 tbsp superfine sugar
¼ tsp ground cinnamon
4 wheat tortillas (see page 12)
¼ cup butter
sifted confectioners' sugar
¼ cup slivered almonds, toasted

1 Halve the paw-paw, scoop out the seeds, peel, and cut into small dice; or peel and dice the guavas; or peel the mango, remove the pit, and dice the flesh. Slice the strawberries. Put the fruit into a bowl.

2 Finely grate half the rind from the orange, and add to the fruit. Cut away the peel and pith from the orange, and ease out the segments from between the membranes. Cut the segments in half, and mix with the fruit, adding the sugar and cinnamon.

3 Divide the mixture between the tortillas, placing on one side; then fold in half, and in half again to make a quarter or pocket.

4 Melt half the butter in a small pan and fry the chimichangas 2 at a time for 1–2 minutes on each side until golden-brown, turning them over carefully. Place on warmed plates, then add the remaining butter to the pan, and fry the other 2 chimichangas in the same way.

5 Sift confectioner's sugar over the chimichangas, and sprinkle them with the toasted slivered almonds. Serve them hot.

OTHER FRUITS

Other fruits such as raspberries and cherries can be used for this recipe instead of the tropical fruits.

MEXICAN BREAD PUDDING

This is somewhat different from the bread pudding we know, though it still contains raisins, nuts, orange rind, and spices, together with toasted French bread soaked in a syrup, and a layer of sharp cheese. The whole mixture is encased and baked in tortillas.

STEP 3

STEP 4

STEP 5

STEP 6

SERVES 6

1 small French stick
1¹/₄ cups butter

SYRUP:
1 cup soft brown sugar
scant 1 cup water
1 cinnamon stick
6 whole cloves or a good pinch of ground
 cloves
¹/₄ tsp apple pie spice
1¹/₄ cups milk
3–4 wheat or corn tortillas (7–8 inches)
 (see page 12)
1 cup raisins
³/₄ cup almonds, slivered or chopped
grated rind of 1 orange
generous ¹/₂ cup grated sharp Cheddar cheese

1 Cut the French stick into ½-in. slices (about 14), and spread each side lightly with some of the butter. Place on a baking sheet, and cook in a preheated oven at 350°F for about 10 minutes, or until golden-brown.

2 Meanwhile, make the syrup: put the soft brown sugar and water into a saucepan with the cinnamon stick, whole or ground cloves, and apple pie spice. Heat gently until dissolved, and then simmer for 2 minutes. Strain into a jug, discarding the spices, and then mix in the milk.

3 Use the remaining butter to grease an ovenproof dish of about 7-cup capacity. Use the tortillas to line the dish, cutting them to fit neatly.

4 Dip half the baked bread slices into the syrup, and lay over the tortillas in the dish.

5 Combine the raisins, almonds, and orange rind, and sprinkle half over the bread, followed by half the grated cheese.

6 Dip the remaining slices of bread in the syrup, and lay over the raisin mixture; then sprinkle with the remaining raisins, nuts, and cheese.

7 Pour the remaining syrup into the dish, and place in a preheated oven at 400°F for 20 minutes. Reduce the temperature to 325°F, cover with a sheet of baking parchment or foil, and continue to cook for about 30 minutes. Serve the bread pudding hot, warm, or cold cut into wedges, with cream, ice cream, or natural yogurt.

STEP 1

STEP 2

STEP 3

STEP 4

CINNAMON BAKED CUSTARD

This dish, similar to the familiar crème caramel, is called a flan in Mexico, and is made in either individual pots or in one large container to be turned out before eating. Serve plain or with cream.

SERVES 6

³/₄ cup superfine sugar
3 tbsp water

CUSTARD:
5 eggs
3 tbsp superfine sugar
2¹/₂ cups milk
3 tbsp heavy cream
few drops of vanilla extract
good pinch of ground allspice
¹/₂ tsp ground cinnamon
pouring or whipped cream to serve
*   (optional)*

1 Prepare a 6–7-in. deep round cake pan, or 6 individual ramekin dishes or dariole molds, by rinsing with cold water. Put the sugar into a heavy-bottomed saucepan with the water and mix together. Heat gently, stirring constantly until the sugar has dissolved. Bring to a boil, increase the heat, and boil, uncovered and without stirring it further, until the sugar has turned a golden-brown.

2 Pour the caramel quickly into the large container, or divide between the individual ones, tipping so the caramel coats the base and a little way up the sides of the container(s) evenly. Leave for a few minutes to set.

3 To make the custard, whisk the eggs together lightly with the sugar, then whisk in the milk and cream, and strain into a jug. Whisk the vanilla extract, allspice, and ground cinnamon into the custard, and pour the custard over the caramel.

4 Place the container(s) in a baking pan, and add boiling water to come halfway up the sides of the container(s). Lay a sheet of greased baking parchment or foil over the custard.

5 Place in a preheated oven at 300°F, allowing about 45 minutes for the individual custards, or 1–1¹/₄ hours for the large one, until set and until a knife inserted in the custard comes out clean. Remove from the water bath and let cool; then chill thoroughly.

6 Dip each container briefly in hot water, and let sit for a minute or so. Shake gently to loosen, and invert onto a serving dish or individual plates, letting the caramel flow around the custard. Serve plain or with pouring or whipped cream, if liked.

STEP 1

STEP 2

STEP 3

STEP 4

VANILLA & CINNAMON ICE CREAM

This rich, creamy ice cream flavored with vanilla and cinnamon has an added tang from the addition of crème fraîche; chopped toasted nuts can also be added. Serve with fresh fruits or a chocolate sauce.

SERVES 4–6

4 eggs
$\frac{1}{4}$ cup superfine sugar
scant 2 cups milk
few drops of vanilla extract
1 tsp ground cinnamon
scant 1 cup crème fraîche or $1\frac{1}{4}$ cups heavy
    cream
3 tbsp toasted chopped hazelnuts or almonds
    (optional)
fresh fruits to decorate

1 To make the custard, whisk the eggs with the sugar until thick in a heatproof bowl. Heat the milk to just below boiling point, and whisk into the egg mixture gradually.

2 Stand the bowl over a pan of gently simmering water, and cook over a low heat, stirring almost constantly until thickened sufficiently to coat the back of a spoon quite thickly. Remove from the heat, and stir in the vanilla extract and cinnamon. Cover with plastic wrap, and leave until cold.

3 If using crème fraîche, just mix evenly through the custard; or if using heavy cream, whip until thick but not too stiff, and fold into the custard.

Cover the bowl, or pour into a loaf pan, and freeze until just firm.

4 Remove the ice cream from the freezer, and whisk until smooth, transferring to a bowl if necessary. This breaks down the ice crystals in the ice cream. Beat in the nuts, if using.

5 Cover, return to the freezer, and freeze until firm. (An ice cream maker may be used if available.)

6 Serve the ice cream spooned into bowls, and decorated with fresh fruits such as strawberries, raspberries, mangoes, or guavas; or top with a chocolate sauce.

CHOCOLATE SAUCE

To make chocolate sauce, melt 4 squares dark chocolate with 2 tablespoons of butter in a bowl and beat in scant 1 cup of evaporated milk and a few drops of vanilla extract until smooth, heating a little if necessary to remove any lumps. 1–2 tablespoons brandy or rum may also be added.

STEP 1

STEP 2

STEP 4

STEP 5

CHURROS (SPICED FRITTERS)

Light orange-flavored fritters, similar to choux puffs, are tossed in aniseed-flavored sugar and served hot or cold with a cinnamon syrup.

SERVES 4–6

¹/₄ cup butter
²/₃ cup water
¹/₂ cup plus 2 tbsp all-purpose flour, sifted
2 eggs, beaten
grated rind of ¹/₂ orange
oil for deep-frying

ANISEED SUGAR:
5 star anise
¹/₃ cup superfine sugar

CINNAMON SYRUP:
²/₃ cup soft brown sugar
²/₃ cup water
2 star anise
¹/₂ tsp ground cinnamon
2 tbsp orange juice

1 Melt the butter in the water in a saucepan over a gentle heat; then bring to a boil. Add the flour all at once, stirring vigorously over a low heat until the mixture forms a ball, leaving the sides of the pan clean. Remove from the heat, and let cool for 4–5 minutes.

2 To make the aniseed sugar, put the star anise and sugar into a pestle and mortar, a food processor, or a blender, and grind until well mixed. Sift into a bowl.

3 To make the cinnamon syrup, put the brown sugar into a small pan with the water, star anise, and cinnamon, and heat until the sugar dissolves; then boil for about 2 minutes. Stir in the orange juice, and strain into a jug.

4 Add the beaten eggs gradually to the cooling choux paste, beating hard (preferably with an electric hand mixer) until smooth and glossy. The mixture may not take quite all the egg. Beat in the orange rind, and put the choux paste into a large piping bag fitted with a large star tip.

5 Heat the oil to 350°F or until a cube of bread browns in about a minute. Pipe 1–1½-in. lengths of the choux paste carefully into the hot oil, cutting each one off with a knife, and fry about 6 at a time for about 3–4 minutes, or until they are golden-brown and crisp all over.

6 Drain the churros on paper towels, then toss thoroughly in the aniseed sugar, and serve hot, warm, or cold with the cinnamon syrup.

MEXICAN CUISINE

CHILIS

As a rough guide, the smaller they are, the hotter they are.

Green chilis are often hotter than red varieties.

The seeds and white veins are the hottest part of all, but have less flavor, so are usually removed before use.

Never put your fingers near your eyes after touching a cut chili, as they will really burn. Always treat chilis with great care.

Dried chilis are fairly mild in flavor, reddish-brown, and well-wrinkled.

Types of chili

Jalapeño chilis are rich, dark green, and hot to very hot, and are also available canned or in a jar. Serrano chilis are small, light green, and extremely hot. Mulato, Ancho, and Pasilla chilies are all dark brownish-black, rather wrinkled, fruity, and slightly sweet with varying degrees of hotness.

Chili powder

This is made up of ground dried chilis, and often includes ground cumin, salt, and a few other spices in small quantities. Each specific make will vary slightly, but it is possible to buy hot, medium, and mild varieties of chili powder. Always add sparingly – it is very powerful.

THE HISTORY OF MEXICAN COOKING

The cuisine of Mexico, though it has changed over the years, remains one that is based on age-old recipes that use the staple foods of the old country – chiefly corn, beans of all kinds, potatoes and sweet potatoes, avocados, tomatoes, chilis, pumpkin, turkey and duck, a wealth of fish from the long coastline, and the delicious cinnamon-flavored chocolate. Over the centuries, traditional Mexican recipes were combined with the comparatively new influences brought by the conquering Spaniards in the sixteenth century, who arrived with the cattle (for milk and meat), poultry, pigs, wheat, rice, citrus fruits, and spices. The combination of the two methods of cooking soon brought forth a wonderful array of new dishes, though they were still based on the old ideas of the Aztecs and Mayans, enhanced with Spanish touches and produce.

SIMPLE RECIPES

Mexican food is easy to prepare at home. With a few exceptions, most of the recipes are uncomplicated and fairly quick to put together. Garnishes and decorations are kept to a minimum, and the food is prepared in a relaxed manner that reflects the informal nature of Mexican cuisine. Of course there are certain skills required for a few of the dishes, and the making of the tortilla is probably the most important to master.

Tortillas

The tortilla is really the staple bread of Mexico. Traditionally, it is made with maize meal (masa harina), but can also be made with wheat flour or with a combination of the two, which is becoming more popular in the north of the country near to the US border. Maize meal is finely ground corn, pale yellow in color and available in health-food stores and some supermarkets. It is sometimes called cornmeal, but it is not the same thing as either polenta or cornstarch.

The dough must be properly prepared, rested, and then rolled out thickly into a circle, or you can use a tortilla press to make the perfect tortilla. If you have problems rolling the dough into a circle, trim it around a suitably sized plate.

Tortillas are cooked for the minimum length of time on a heated "cormal" or heavy-bottomed skillet, which should be heated slowly and evenly before the tortilla is added; the tortilla is cooked until just speckled brown, then flipped over to cook the second side. If bubbles appear in the surface, they should be pressed down with a rolled-up dish cloth or pad of paper towels. The pan should not be greased unless the tortillas stick – normally they do not – and then only lightly with a touch of oil. When made, wrap in a clean dish cloth. If left uncovered, they will immediately firm up. To store them for future use, layer a piece of nonstick baking parchment between each tortilla, and wrap in a clean dish cloth, then put in either a polythene bag or airtight container, and chill for up to 3 days. If they become firm, they can be reheated in a pan, fried, or dipped briefly in boiling water to soften, so that they can then be further shaped or rolled, and used for making other dishes. Tortillas are eaten as a dish in themselves, and are also used as the base for a variety of dishes, including Burritos, Tostados, Tacos, Tortilla Chips, Nachos, Enchiladas, and Quesadillas.

Chilis

Many people think that all Mexican food is red-hot and almost inedible unless you have a stomach of iron. True, it is highly spiced, and chilis certainly appear in abundance in recipes, but the amount and type of chilis used governs both the spiciness and "hotness" of the dish, so it is up to the cook to decide just how much or how little to add. There are several types of chili that are commonly used. However, some of them are readily available only in Mexico and similar countries, so in the recipes I have only stipulated chilis – you can use which-ever type you prefer, or is available.

Beans

Another important ingredient in the Mexican diet is the bean, particularly the pinkish pinto bean, the black bean, and the red kidney bean. Both fresh and dried beans are used widely to serve as "stewed" or "pot" beans as an everyday dish. Long, slow cooking is essential to make the beans digestible, and salt should be added only when they are tender, or the beans will take forever to tenderize. Many flavors can be added

during cooking, including onions, chilis, bacon, garlic, and many others, which the beans readily absorb.

Each type of bean has its own special quality and flavor, and every family will have its own particular way of cooking them, either to be eaten as they are, or to be turned into Refried Beans. This is another traditional (and famous) Mexican dish, which can be eaten as a dish in its own right, or it can form part of many other Mexican dishes, particularly in combination with tortillas and their various fillings and toppings. Stewed or pot beans (or drained canned beans) are added to fried onion, garlic, and chili, mashed as they are added, and then cooked to a thick paste to serve either hot or cold.

Salads

Guacamole and Tomato Salsa are regular accompaniments to many Mexican dishes, and are flavored with chilis and onions; they are very attractive and tasty, and can be eaten alone as well as being presented as a side dish to other foods. Other salads tend to use a mixture of fruit and vegetables, often combining flavors we may not be accustomed to, but which turn out to blend extremely well. For instance, beetroot, bananas, mangoes, and pomegranates are often mixed with a range of vegetables, giving the finished dish color, texture, and an original flavor.

Bell peppers

Bell peppers feature extensively in Mexican cookery, in all varieties and colors, including red, green, orange, and

OTHER INGREDIENTS

Cheese in Mexican cooking
Use a white crumbly cheese such as Cheshire or Greek Feta as the best substitutes for the salty Mexican cheeses; or use a mixture of Mozzarella and sharp Cheddar.

Cooking fats
Good pork fat is most widely used in Mexico in cooking, but vegetable oils and butter make good substitutes.

Cream
Cream in Mexico is similar to the French crème fraîche, but is often difficult to find. To make your own, add 1 tbsp of natural yogurt to 1¼ cups whipping cream and leave overnight, or add 2 tsps buttermilk to 1¼ cups double cream and leave at room temperature for up to 24 hours until thickened, and then refrigerate. Alternatively, use soured cream.

Tomatoes
In Mexico, tomatoes grow large and unevenly shaped, similar to beefsteak or Mediterranean varieties. For the most authentic Mexican shaped and flavored tomatoes, use those sun-ripened in the garden, not grown in a greenhouse.

Star anise
This is the dried star-shaped fruit of an evergreen tree with a strong aniseed flavor.

USING A TORTILLA PRESS

These are available from specialist kitchen equipment shops and larger department stores. They ensure evenly shaped and thin tortillas all of a regular size, something that takes time and a lot of practice to achieve by hand.

Line the base of the press with a square of greaseproof, non-stick baking parchment. Flatten a piece of tortilla dough about the size of a small egg, then place on the paper and cover with another piece of paper. Close the press, pushing down the handle firmly.

Open the press, remove the top piece of paper and invert the tortilla on to a hot griddle, or stack up between damp cloths, or put into an airtight container until ready to cook.

HANDY TIP

Enriching stews

To enrich an already well-flavored and rich meat stew or casserole, add 1–1½ squares Mexican chocolate or bittersweet chocolate and a pinch of ground cinnamon, stirring until well melted and absorbed into the juices.

yellow. Some people find the taste of pepper can be harsh and almost bitter. To remove this, the Mexicans always roast or toast the pepper to peel the skin, which in turn takes away any bitterness. It is simple to do. First cut the pepper in half from stem to tip, and lay the pieces, cut-side down, on a foil-lined grill rack, and cook under a moderate heat until the skin chars and turns completely black. Remove and let cool a little. The skin will then peel off easily. Finally, turn over the pepper, and remove the stem, membrane and any seeds, and it is ready for use. Peppers may also be dry-fried by placing each half, skin-side down, in a "cormal" or heavy-bottomed skillet and cooked slowly over a low heat until the skin blisters and chars.

Tomatoes

Tomatoes are an important part of Mexican cuisine, as they are used in salads – including the indispensable Tomato Salsa – as well as in a great many main-course dishes and a wide range of sauces. If they are to be cooked or added to cooked dishes, the skins are always removed first. This can be done in either of two ways. One is to place the tomatoes in a bowl, and cover them with boiling water for a minute; then make a nick in the skin with a knife, and transfer them quickly to a bowl of cold water. The skin will then peel off easily. If you have a gas stove top, you can impale the tomato on a long fork, and hold it carefully over the flame, turning it so that it heats evenly, until the skin chars and splits, after which it will peel off easily. This can also be done by placing the tomato under

a hot broiler until the skin just chars and splits.

Cilantro

Also known as Chinese parsley and coriander, cilantro is used in many Mexican recipes, either as a flavoring ingredient or as a garnish. It has a fairly potent but refreshing flavor, and is a true taste of Mexico. However, it does wilt extremely easily, so should be picked fresh or kept in cold water until it is used.

Coriander seeds and ground coriander are also used in Mexican cuisine, but the flavors are quite different, and fresh cilantro and seed coriander are not interchangeable.

Spices

Several spices feature frequently in Mexican recipes, particularly cumin and cinnamon. Cumin, either in seed or powdered form, gives a touch of the oriental flavor brought by Indian settlers; cinnamon, used both ground and in stick form, is found in both sweet and savory dishes. Mexican chocolate is flavored with cinnamon also, and if you use any other type of chocolate for a Mexican recipe, it is advisable to add a pinch of ground cinnamon for an authentic taste. Cloves too are used frequently in Mexican dishes, often in their ground form.

Pumpkin seeds

When the skin is removed from pumpkin seeds, the familiar green seeds are revealed, which are known as "pepitas." They can be added to dishes as they are, or they can be toasted or roasted first.

Often ground up to make a dip or dressing, they have a delicious nutty flavor and are extremely nutritious. If you cannot find them in your local supermarket, they are usually available from health-food stores.

Tacos

These can be bought ready-made in airtight packages and are often eaten as a snack – the Mexican version of potato chips. They can easily be made at home simply by cutting homemade tortillas into wedges, and frying them in deep or shallow fat until they are crispy. They are ideal for serving with dips such as Guacamole, as the dips complement the dry hot taste of the tacos. When fried, they can be kept for up to a week in an airtight container.

Mexican drinks

There are several drinks associated with Mexico, most of which are pretty, and ideal for a party. Everyone knows the famous Tequila Sunrise – a mixture of tequila, orange juice, a touch of grenadine, and lime juice, served with crushed ice. The Margarita is perhaps equally famous; it is a blend of tequila, lime juice, clear orange liqueur such as Cointreau, and crushed ice.

Every country has its own version of fresh lemonade and in Mexico it is particularly refreshing; but whether or not you ever visit Mexico and try the lemonade, you must sample their hot chocolate. Put 3 cups of milk into a saucepan with 3 thin strips of orange rind. Bring barely to a boil, remove from the heat, cover and let sit for 5 minutes;

then discard the rind. Blend 3 squares of Mexican chocolate or plain dark chocolate with a good pinch of ground cinnamon with the milk until dissolved, and whisk until the mixture is really frothy. Serve at once, topped with a pinch of ground cinnamon – quite delicious!

Freezing

On the whole, Mexican food is not very suitable for freezing, mainly because of the strong flavors involved – particularly chilis and chili sauces, which are widely used. When strong flavors are frozen they tend to intensify, and if left for more than a couple of weeks, a musty flavor can develop which spoils the dish, although it is not harmful to health. So before you decide to freeze a dish, consider whether it is really going to be helpful, and do so only if necessary and then for just a couple of weeks. Tortillas, which are widely used in Mexican cuisine, cannot be frozen, so this does make many of the recipes unsuitable for freezing as they feature in them so frequently.

Mexican food is very distinctive, but with its simplicity and the wide use of fresh local produce you will find, as many people do, that the flavors and spiciness can quickly become almost addictive. Whether you want to serve a complete Mexican meal, or intersperse your cooking with an appetizer, main dish, or dessert with a Mexican flavor, or just serve one of the delicious snacks, you are sure to be pleasantly surprised by the simplicity of the preparation and the mouth-watering results.

SALSA VERDE

An alternative to Tomato Salsa (see page 24), this salad makes an attractive and different accompaniment to Mexican dishes.

1 pound tomatillos or green
    tomatoes, chopped
$^1/_2$ medium onion, chopped very
    finely
1 level tbsp fresh cilantro,
    chopped
salt and pepper

Mix well, turn into a bowl and cover with plastic food wrap. Chill for at least 30 minutes.

MEXICAN SALAD DRESSING

6 tbsps sunflower oil, or olive oil,
    or a mixture of the two
2 tbsps white wine vinegar
$^1/_2$ level tsp Dijon mustard
pinch granulated sugar
1–2 level tbsps fresh cilantro,
    chopped
salt and pepper

1. Put all the ingredients into a screw-top jar. Shake well until emulsified.

2. Store for 3–4 days in the refrigerator.

3. Without the addition of the fresh cilantro, the dressing will keep for up to 10 days – just add the herb before serving.

INDEX